Become an Earned Value Management Expert in One day

Dedications

This book is dedicated to God almighty for the enablement and inspiration to write , my family for their support and encouragement especially, my baby David who made every situation joyful; and for you who is committed to delivering projects effectively to achieve set goals by minimising cost overrun and schedule slip.

Table of Contents

Preface

Having spent over 20 years with versatile experience in project cost estimation, project scope development, delivery/execution, monitoring,benchmarking and review. I have practical knowledge on why many projects globally are abandoned, budget overrun and eventually fail to achieve project set objectives and goals.

This book is written out of my passion for successful projects to provide you with applicable practical calculated examples and how to apply the examples on your day to day project and specific EVM metrics to monitor cost and schedule effectively at the lowest project package/task at a glance without jargons.

With this book , you will excel better in managing and monitoring projects, your project will no longer overrun its cost or schedule delayed without identification at the earliest time for remedial/corrective action to be taken to minimise the impact and ripple effect.

Chapter 1: Introduction to Earned Value Management (EVM)

Welcome to the world of Earned Value Management (EVM)! In this book, we will embark on a journey to explore the fundamental concepts, principles, and techniques of EVM, an invaluable metrics in project management performance measure. Whether you're new to project management or seeking to enhance your skills, this book will provide you with a solid foundation in EVM.

Earned Value Management (EVM) is a project management technique that integrates schedule, cost, and scope metrics to provide a comprehensive view of project performance. It allows project managers and controllers to monitor and report on the progress and health of a project by comparing planned performance against actual performance. The benefits of using EVM include early identification of project issues, improved decision-making, accurate forecasting, and enhanced communication with stakeholders. EMV is an effective and efficient method to assess total project cost and schedule performance It helps to identify potential issues, and risk early before it occurs for preventive and remedial actions to be implemented. EVM is ideal for all projects but very valuable for monitoring and controlling complex and capital projects.

EVM key metrics:

Planned Value (PV): Is the authorised budget or baseline cost assigned to scheduled work to be completed at a given time. It shows how much work should have been accomplished at a given point in time. It is also called Budgeted Cost of Work Scheduled (BCWS). This metric is used to evaluate if a project has achieved its planned target at the specified time in terms of schedule and cost.

Earned Value (EV): Is the value of work actually performed or completed up to a specific date. Also, called Budgeted Cost Work Performed (BCWP). EV is typically measured in monetary terms. The formula to calculate EV is EV = BAC* Actual % of work complete. BAC is Budget at Completion, Actual% is the actual percentage of work completed up to the period date. EV metric is used to assess the value achieved relative to the Planned Value (PV).

Actual Cost (AC): Is the total cost incurred in completing the work up to a specific date. It is also referred to as Actual Cost Of Work Performed (ACWP). Is an important metric used to identify if cost is being overrun or underrun. When comparing PV and EV.

Schedule Variance (SV): SV measures the schedule performance by comparing the difference between earned value (EV) and planned value (PV). it shows deviation from plan.
The formula for SV is SV = EV - PV. A positive SV means the project is ahead of planned schedule.

Cost Variance (CV): This measures the cost performance by comparing the difference between earned value (EV) and actual cost (AC) and shows deviation.The formula for CV is CV = EV - AC. A positive CV means cost savings and suggests more work completed than planned.

Cost Performance Index (CPI): This metric is used to measure project cost efficiency. Tracking project CPI will help manage costs effectively and remedial actions taken on time.

Formula to calculate CPI =EV/AC.

- CPI >1,indicates project is under budget
- CPI<1, indicates project is over budget
- CPI =1 indicates project is on budget

Schedule Performance Index (SPI): this metric is used to evaluate/measure schedule performance, monitoring this metric, will help identify schedule slip/deviation from plan.

- SPI >1,indicates project is ahead of planned schedule
- SPI<1, indicates project is behind planned schedule
- SPI =1 indicates project is on schedule as planned

Now, let's see how these calculations and metrics can provide insights into project monitoring and reporting:

Performance Measurement: EVM allows project managers/controllers to measure the performance of the project in terms of schedule and cost. SV and CV provide valuable information on whether the project is ahead or behind schedule and whether it is over or under budget. Positive SV and CV values indicate favourable performance, while negative values indicate unfavourable performance.

Trend Analysis: By calculating SV and CV over time, project managers can identify trends and patterns in project performance. They can analyse whether the project is consistently performing well or if there are recurring issues that need to be addressed.

Forecasting: EVM enables accurate forecasting of project outcomes based on past performance. By extrapolating SV and CV trends, project managers can estimate the project's future performance and make necessary adjustments to meet project objectives.

Early Issue Identification: EVM metrics help in early identification of project issues. If SV or CV shows significant deviations from the planned values, it alerts project managers to potential problems, allowing them to take corrective actions promptly.

Stakeholder Communication: EVM provides a standardised and objective way to communicate project performance to stakeholders. SV and CV values can be easily **understood and used to convey the project's status, progress, and potential risks.**

Chapter 2: Understanding the Basics Metrics and Calculation

In this chapter, we will delve into the basic concepts of EVM. We'll learn about Planned Value (PV), Earned Value (EV), Actual Cost (AC), and the key metrics derived from these values, such as Schedule Variance (SV) and Cost Variance (CV). Through clear explanations and illustrative examples, you'll gain a deeper understanding of how these metrics are calculated and interpreted.

Assuming you are managing a software development project with a budget of $100,000 and a planned duration of 10 weeks. After 6 weeks, you assess the following information:

PV (Planned Value): $65,000
EV (Earned Value): $55,000

AC (Actual Cost): $65,000

Calculations:
SV = EV - PV = $55,000 - $65,000 = -$10,000

CV = EV - AC = $55,000 - $65,000 = -$10,000

In this example, the negative SV (-$10,000) indicates that the project is behind schedule, as the earned value is lower than the planned value. The negative CV (-$10,000) suggests that the project is over budget since the actual cost is higher than the earned value.

Based on these metrics, you can identify that the project is facing schedule and cost performance issues, prompting you to take appropriate corrective actions to bring the project back on track.

Overall, EVM provides a comprehensive and objective approach to project monitoring and reporting, helping.

Further calculation of PV, EV, CPI, SPI, interpret metrics when CPI and SPI are less than 1, greater than 1 and equal to 1 and plot graph of the metrics

Follow these steps:

Step 1: Define the project tasks and establish a baseline schedule and budget.

Step 2: Determine the Planned Value (PV):

- Assign a budgeted cost to each task(activity) based on the planned schedule.
- Sum up the budgeted costs to calculate the PV, which represents the authorised budget assigned to scheduled work.

Step 3: Measure the Earned Value (EV):

- Assess the actual progress of each task in monetary terms.
- Sum up the actual progress values to calculate the EV, which represents the value of work completed up to a specific date.

Step 4: Determine the Actual Cost (AC):

- Calculate the total cost incurred in completing the work up to a specific date.

Step 5: Calculate Schedule Variance (SV):

- SV = EV - PV
- SV measures the schedule performance by comparing the difference between EV and PV.
- A positive SV indicates that the project is ahead of schedule, while a negative SV indicates it is behind schedule.

Step 6: Calculate Cost Variance (CV):

- CV = EV - AC
- CV measures the cost performance by comparing the difference between EV and AC.
- A positive CV indicates that the project is under budget, while a negative CV indicates it is over budget.

Step 7: Calculate Cost Performance Index (CPI):

- CPI = EV / AC

- CPI reflects the cost efficiency of the project. It indicates how efficiently the project team is utilising the budget.
- A CPI greater than 1 indicates the project is performing well within the budget, while a CPI less than 1 indicates cost overrun.

Step 8: Calculate Schedule Performance Index (SPI):

- SPI = EV / PV
- SPI reflects the schedule efficiency of the project. It indicates how efficiently the project team is progressing against the planned schedule.
- An SPI greater than 1 indicates the project is ahead of schedule, while an SPI less than 1 indicates schedule delays.

Interpret the metrics:

CPI less than 1: When the CPI is less than 1, it means the project cost is over budget. The project team is spending more than what is earned (More cost incurred for tasks completed more than budgeted). It indicates a cost overrun, and corrective actions need to be taken to bring the project back on track financially.

CPI greater than 1: When the CPI is greater than 1, it means the project is under budget. The project team is spending less than what is earned (less cost incurred for completed task less than budgeted). It indicates that the project is cost-efficient and performing well within the allocated budget.

CPI equal to 1: When the CPI is equal to 1, it means the project is exactly on budget. The project team is spending exactly what is earned, indicating a balanced financial performance.

SPI less than 1: When the SPI is less than 1, it means the project is behind schedule. The project team is progressing slower than planned. Corrective actions should be taken to address the delays and ensure timely completion.

SPI greater than 1: When the SPI is greater than 1, it means the project is ahead of schedule. The project team is progressing faster than planned. It indicates a favourable schedule performance and may provide opportunities for project acceleration or resource reallocation.

To plot a graph of the metrics, you can create a time-based chart with the x-axis representing the project timeline (weeks, months, etc.) and the y-axis representing the values of PV, EV, CPI, and SPI. Each metric can be plotted as a line graph, allowing you to visualise the trend and performance over time.

Table1: Example calculated metrics PV, EV, AC and CPI and SPI index for a project 10 weeks duration

We now look at the table below for PV, EV, CPI, and SPI for a project over a timeline of 10 weeks. We will assume the following values:

Table 1: Calculated Metrics

Week	PV ($)	EV ($)	AC ($)	CPI (EV / AC)	SPI (EV / PV)
1	1200	600	700	0.86	0.50
2	2200	1600	1700	0.94	0.73
3	3200	2100	2500	0.84	0.66
4	4200	4100	3800	1.05	1.05
5	5200	5600	5200	1.08	1.08
6	6200	6600	6700	0.99	1.10
7	7200	7100	7100	1.01	1.01
8	8200	8200	7900	1.04	1.00
9	9200	9200	8900	1.03	1.00
10	10000	9500	9800	0.97	0.95

Interpretation:

Remember:

- PV represents the planned value, showing the authorised budget assigned to scheduled work.
- EV represents the earned value, indicating the value of work completed up to a specific date.
- CPI represents the cost performance index, reflecting the cost efficiency of the project.
- SPI represents the schedule performance index, reflecting the schedule efficiency of the project.

From the Table values, we can observe the following:

- In the early weeks, both CPI and SPI are less than 1, indicating cost overruns and schedule delays. The project is not performing efficiently in terms of budget and schedule.
- Around Week 4, both CPI and SPI reach or exceed 1, indicating improved cost performance and schedule adherence.
- In the later weeks, CPI fluctuates around 1, indicating that the project remains on budget. However, SPI drops below 1 again in week 10, indicating schedule delays.

Chapter 3: Setting Up Your Project for EVM

Before diving into EVM implementation, it's essential to set up your project effectively. In this chapter, we'll discuss the importance of establishing a solid project plan, defining work packages, assigning resources, and establishing a baseline schedule and budget. You'll learn how proper project planning lays the groundwork for successful EVM implementation

Setting up a project for Earned Value Management (EVM) involves several key steps to ensure that you have a solid foundation for implementing EVM techniques effectively. Let's walk through these steps with examples:

1. Define the Project Scope:

Before anything else, it's crucial to clearly define the scope of your project. This involves identifying the objectives, deliverables, constraints, and assumptions of the project.

Example: Suppose you're tasked with developing a new software application for a client. The scope of the project includes defining the features and functionalities of the software, as well as any specific requirements provided by the client.

2. Break Down the Work Structure:

Break down the project work into smaller, manageable components or work packages. This breakdown helps in organising and planning the project activities effectively.

Example: For the software development project, you might break down the work structure into components such as user interface design, database development, backend programming, testing, and documentation.

3. Develop a Work Breakdown Structure (WBS):

Create a hierarchical representation of the project work breakdown structure, showing how the work packages are organised and related to each other.

Example:Mobile Application development project, the WBS sample:

1 Mobile Application Development Project
1.1 Project Management
1.2 User Interface Design
1.3 Database Development
1.4 Appy Development
1.5 Quality Assurance
1.6 Deployment and Maintenance
1.7 Documentation

4. Assign Resources and Estimates:

Identify the resources (human, financial, and material) required for each work package and estimate the time and cost associated with completing them.

Example: For the software development project, you might allocate specific developers, designers, and testers to each work package and estimate the hours required for completion based on their expertise and past experience.

5. Establish Baseline Schedule and Budget:

Develop a baseline schedule and budget for the project, incorporating the planned start and end dates for each work package and the associated costs.

Example: Based on the resource allocations and estimates, you create a project schedule that outlines the start and end dates for each phase of the software development process. You also establish a budget that includes the costs for personnel, equipment, and any other expenses.

6. Define Performance Measurement Baseline (PMB):

Establish the Performance Measurement Baseline (PMB), which includes the planned values (PV) for each work package, representing the authorised budget assigned to scheduled work.

Example: Using the software development project, you assign budgeted costs to each work package based on the planned schedule. For instance, you allocate $10,000 for User Interface Design, $15,000 for Database Development, and so on.

By following these steps and examples, you can effectively set up your project for Earned Value Management (EVM). Having a well-defined scope, work breakdown structure, resource allocations, baseline schedule, and budget provides the groundwork for implementing EVM techniques and monitoring project performance accurately.

Based on this analysis, you would need to take corrective actions to address the schedule delays and cost overruns to bring the project back on track.

Chapter 4: Implementing EVM in Your Project

Now that we've laid the groundwork, it's time to implement EVM in your project. We'll walk through the step-by-step process of applying EVM techniques, from tracking progress and collecting data to calculating key metrics such as SV, CV, SPI, and CPI. You'll gain practical insights into how EVM can help you monitor project performance effectively.

Implementing EVM in Your Project and examples

Implementing Earned Value Management (EVM) in your project involves several steps to track project performance effectively. Let's go through the process with examples:

1. Define Work Packages:

Break down the project work into smaller, manageable components or work packages.

Example: For a construction project, work packages could include foundation laying, framing, electrical installation, plumbing, roofing, etc.

2. Assign Budgets and Schedules:

Assign budgets and schedules to each work package based on the project plan.

Example: Suppose the budget for the framing work package is $20,000, and the scheduled duration is 4 weeks.

3. Measure Progress:

Track the progress of each work package to determine the earned value (EV), representing the value of work completed.

Example: After 2 weeks, you assess that 50% of the framing work has been completed. Therefore, the EV for the framing work package is $10,000.

4. Track Actual Costs:

Record the actual costs incurred for each work package to determine the actual cost (AC).

Example: After 2 weeks, you find that the actual cost incurred for framing is $12,000.

5. Calculate EVM Metrics:

Calculate key EVM metrics such as Schedule Variance (SV), Cost Variance (CV), Cost Performance Index (CPI), and Schedule Performance Index (SPI) based on the EV, PV, and AC.

- Schedule Variance (SV): SV = EV - PV
- Cost Variance (CV): CV = EV - AC
- Cost Performance Index (CPI): CPI = EV / AC
- Schedule Performance Index (SPI): SPI = EV / PV

Example:

- For the framing work package:
    - PV = $20,000 (Planned Budget)
    - EV = $10,000 (Earned Value)
    - AC = $12,000 (Actual Cost)
- Calculate SV: SV = EV - PV = $10,000 - $20,000 = -$10,000 (Behind schedule)
- Calculate CV: CV = EV - AC = $10,000 - $12,000 = -$2,000 (Over budget)
- Calculate CPI: CPI = EV / AC = $10,000 / $12,000 ≈ 0.83 (Cost efficiency is below target)
- Calculate SPI: SPI = EV / PV = $10,000 / $20,000 = 0.50 (Schedule efficiency is below target)

6. Analyse and Interpret Metrics:

Interpret the EVM metrics to gain insights into project performance and identify areas requiring attention.

Example: Based on the calculations, you find that the framing work package is behind schedule and over budget. The cost efficiency (CPI) and schedule efficiency (SPI) are both below target. This indicates that corrective actions are needed to address the delays and cost overruns in the framing work package.

7. Take Corrective Actions:

Based on the analysis, implement corrective actions to bring the project back on track and ensure that future work adheres to the planned schedule and budget.

Example: To address the delays and cost overruns in the framing work package, you may allocate additional resources, adjust the work schedule, or streamline the construction process.

By following these steps and examples, you can effectively implement Earned Value Management (EVM) in your project to monitor performance, identify issues, and take timely corrective actions to ensure project success.

Chapter 5: Analysing EVM Metrics

In this chapter, we'll focus on analysing EVM metrics to gain insights into project performance. We'll explore scenarios where SV, CV, SPI, and CPI are greater than 1, less than 1, or equal to 1, and discuss the implications of each scenario. You'll learn how to interpret EVM metrics to identify project issues, make informed decisions, and communicate effectively with stakeholders.

Analysing EVM Metrics and examples

Analysing Earned Value Management (EVM) metrics is crucial for gaining insights into project performance and identifying areas that require attention. Let's discuss the key EVM metrics and examples of how to analyse them:

1. Schedule Variance (SV):

- Definition: SV measures the schedule performance by comparing the difference between earned value (EV) and planned value (PV).
- Formula: $SV = EV - PV$
- Interpretation:
    - $SV > 0$: The project is ahead of schedule.
    - $SV = 0$: The project is on schedule.
    - $SV < 0$: The project is behind schedule.

19

Example:
If the EV for a project is $50,000 and the PV is $60,000, then the SV would be:
SV = $50,000 - $60,000 = -$10,000

Interpretation: The project is behind schedule by $10,000.

2. Cost Variance (CV):

- Definition: CV measures the cost performance by comparing the difference between earned value (EV) and actual cost (AC).
- Formula: CV = EV - AC
- Interpretation:
    - CV > 0: The project is under budget.
    - CV = 0: The project is on budget.
    - CV < 0: The project is over budget.

Example:
If the EV for a project is $50,000 and the AC is $45,000, then the CV would be:
CV = $50,000 - $45,000 = $5,000

Interpretation: The project is under budget by $5,000.

3. Cost Performance Index (CPI):

- Definition: CPI reflects the cost efficiency of the project, indicating how efficiently the project team is utilising the budget.
- Formula: CPI = EV / AC
- Interpretation:
    - CPI > 1: The project is cost-efficient.
    - CPI = 1: The project is spending exactly as planned.
    - CPI < 1: The project is over budget.

Example:
If the EV for a project is $50,000 and the AC is $45,000, then the CPI would be:
CPI = $50,000 / $45,000 = 1.11

Interpretation: The project is utilising the budget efficiently, with a CPI of 1.11.

4. Schedule Performance Index (SPI):

- Definition: SPI reflects the schedule efficiency of the project, indicating how efficiently the project team is progressing against the planned schedule.
- Formula: SPI = EV / PV

- Interpretation:
  - SPI > 1: The project is ahead of schedule.
  - SPI = 1: The project is progressing exactly as planned.
  - SPI < 1: The project is behind schedule.

Example:
If the EV for a project is $50,000 and the PV is $60,000, then the SPI would be:
SPI = $50,000 / $60,000 = 0.83

Interpretation: The project is behind schedule, with an SPI of 0.83.

5. Analysing EVM Metrics:

- By analysing SV and CV, you can determine whether the project is ahead or behind schedule and whether it's under or over budget.
- CPI and SPI provide insights into cost and schedule efficiency, respectively, indicating how well the project team is performing against the planned objectives.
- Comparing these metrics over time helps identify trends and patterns in project performance and allows for timely corrective actions if needed.

Example:

Suppose you're managing a construction project. After Month 3, you analyse the EVM metrics:

- SV = -$8,000
- CV = -$5,000
- CPI = 0.90
- SPI = 0.80

Interpretation:

- The project is behind schedule by $8,000 (negative SV) and over budget by $5,000 (negative CV).
- The cost efficiency is slightly below target, with a CPI of 0.90.
- The schedule efficiency is below target, with an SPI of 0.80.

Further EVM Calculation examples.

(a). Planned Value (PV):

Planned Value (PV) represents the authorised budget assigned to scheduled work. It shows how much work should have been accomplished at a specific point in time according to the project plan.

Example:
Suppose you're managing a construction project with a total budget of $100,000. According to the project schedule, by the end of Month 1, you planned to complete 25% of the work. Therefore, the Planned Value for Month 1 would be:
PV = Total Budget * Planned Percentage

PV = $100,000 * 25% = $25,000

(b). Earned Value (EV):

Earned Value (EV) represents the value of the work actually performed or completed up to a specific date. It's typically measured in monetary terms.

Example:
Continuing with the construction project example, suppose by the end of Month 1, you've completed 20% of the work, which is less than planned. Therefore, the Earned Value for Month 1 would be:
EV = Total Budget * Actual Percentage

EV = $100,000 * 20% = $20,000

(c). Actual Cost (AC):

Actual Cost (AC) represents the total cost incurred in completing the work up to a specific date. It includes all expenses related to the project.

Example:
For the construction project, suppose by the end of Month 1, you've spent $22,000. Therefore, the Actual Cost for Month 1 would be:

AC = $22,000

(d). Schedule Variance (SV):

Schedule Variance (SV) measures the schedule performance by comparing the difference between earned value (EV) and planned value (PV).

Example:
Using the values from the examples above:
SV = EV - PV
SV = $20,000 - $25,000 = -$5,000

A negative SV indicates that the project is behind schedule.

(e). Cost Variance (CV):

Cost Variance (CV) measures the cost performance by comparing the difference between earned value (EV) and actual cost (AC).

Example:
Using the values from the examples above:
CV = EV - AC
CV = $20,000 - $22,000 = -$2,000

A negative CV indicates that the project is over budget.

These examples illustrate how Planned Value (PV), Earned Value (EV), Actual Cost (AC), Schedule Variance (SV), and Cost Variance (CV) are calculated and used to assess the performance of a project using Earned Value Management.

Chapter 6: Advanced Topics in EVM

As you continue your journey in EVM, it's essential to explore advanced topics that can further enhance your skills. In this chapter, we cover the topics in briefs such as forecasting project outcomes, applying EVM in agile environments, integrating risk management with EVM, and leveraging EVM for portfolio management. You'll gain a deeper understanding of how to apply EVM in complex project scenarios.

Advanced topics in Earned Value Management (EVM) extend beyond the basic concepts and delve into more complex scenarios and applications. Let's explore some of these advanced topics along with an example:

1. Forecasting Project Outcomes:

EVM can be used to forecast project outcomes by extrapolating current performance trends. Forecasting techniques such as To-Complete Performance Index (TCPI) and Estimate at Completion (EAC) help project managers predict the final project cost and schedule based on past performance.

Example: Suppose a software development project is experiencing cost overruns. The project manager calculates the Estimate at Completion (EAC) using different forecasting methods (e.g., EAC = BAC / CPI or EAC = AC + (BAC - EV)) to predict the total project cost and determine if corrective actions are necessary to bring the project back on track.

2. Agile EVM:

Agile methodologies emphasise flexibility and responsiveness to change, making traditional EVM techniques challenging to apply. Agile EVM adapts EVM principles to agile projects by integrating incremental delivery, iterative planning, and frequent feedback loops.

Example: In an agile software development project using Scrum, the team tracks earned value (EV) by assigning points to user stories completed during each sprint. The velocity (average points completed per sprint) is used to estimate the project's progress and forecast future sprints.

3. Integrated Risk Management:

EVM can be integrated with risk management processes to proactively identify, assess, and mitigate project risks. Risk-adjusted EVM techniques consider the impact of risks on project performance metrics and incorporate risk response strategies into the project plan.

Example: In a construction project, the project manager identifies the risk of inclement weather delaying outdoor construction activities. To mitigate this risk, the project schedule includes buffers or contingency reserves to account for potential weather-related delays. Risk-adjusted EVM is used to evaluate the impact of weather risks on project performance metrics and adjust forecasts accordingly.

4. Portfolio Management:

EVM can be applied at the portfolio level to monitor and control multiple projects within an organisation. Portfolio EVM provides stakeholders with visibility into the performance of individual projects and enables resource allocation decisions based on project priorities and strategic objectives.

Example: A large engineering firm manages a portfolio of infrastructure projects, including bridge construction, road expansion, and wastewater treatment plant upgrades. Portfolio EVM is used to aggregate and analyse performance metrics across all projects, identify areas of concern, and optimise resource allocation to maximise overall portfolio performance.

5. Earned Schedule Management:

Earned Schedule Management extends traditional EVM by incorporating schedule performance metrics such as Earned Schedule (ES) and Schedule Performance Index for Time (SPIt). Earned Schedule techniques focus on measuring schedule progress and forecasting project completion dates more accurately.

Example: In a manufacturing project, the project manager uses Earned Schedule Management to assess schedule performance based on the cumulative value of completed work over time. By analysing the Earned Schedule (ES) and Schedule Performance Index for Time (SPIt), the project manager identifies schedule variances and adjusts project plans to meet delivery deadlines.

These advanced topics in Earned Value Management (EVM) provide project managers with additional tools and techniques to address complex project management challenges and optimise project performance in various domains and industries

Chapter 7: Real-World Case Studies

To reinforce your learning, we'll explore real-world case studies where EVM has been successfully applied in various industries and projects. Through these case studies, you'll gain practical insights into how organisations have used EVM to achieve project success, overcome challenges, and deliver value to stakeholders.

Real-World Case Studies and examples

Real-world case studies provide practical examples of how Earned Value Management (EVM) has been successfully applied in various industries and projects. Let's explore some case studies:

1. Construction Project:

Case Study: A large construction company undertook the construction of a high-rise building in a metropolitan area. The project had a tight deadline and a significant budget.

Example: The project team used EVM to monitor progress and control costs throughout the construction phases. By tracking metrics such as Schedule Variance (SV) and Cost Performance Index (CPI), they were able to identify potential delays and cost overruns early. For instance, they discovered that the concrete pouring process was taking longer than planned, leading to schedule delays. By adjusting resource allocation and scheduling additional work shifts, they were able to mitigate the delays and keep the project on track.

2. Software Development Project:

Case Study: A technology company embarked on the development of a new software application to meet market demands. The project involved multiple development teams working in parallel.

Example: EVM was utilised to track the progress of each development team and ensure alignment with the overall project schedule and budget. By analysing metrics such as Earned Value (EV) and Schedule Performance Index (SPI), the project manager identified bottlenecks and resource constraints affecting the project's progress. For example, the testing phase was lagging behind schedule due to a shortage of testing resources. By reallocating resources and streamlining the testing process, the team was able to accelerate progress and deliver the software on time.

3. Aerospace Project:

Case Study: An aerospace company was tasked with developing a new aircraft model, involving complex engineering and manufacturing processes.

Example: EVM was implemented to monitor the performance of the project and ensure compliance with strict budgetary constraints. By analysing metrics such as Cost Variance (CV) and Cost Performance Index (CPI), the project manager identified areas where costs were exceeding budget estimates. For instance, the design phase required additional engineering resources, leading to cost overruns. By reevaluating the design requirements and optimising resource utilisation, the team was able to control costs and bring the project back within budget.

4. Government Project:

Case Study: A government agency initiated a large-scale infrastructure project aimed at improving transportation infrastructure in a region.

Example: EVM was employed to monitor the progress of the project and ensure accountability for taxpayer funds. By tracking metrics such as Planned Value (PV) and Earned Value (EV), stakeholders were able to assess the project's performance against established milestones and deliverables. For instance, the construction of a new highway interchange was behind schedule due to land acquisition delays. By coordinating with local authorities and expediting the land acquisition process, the project team was able to minimise schedule impacts and deliver the project on time.

These case studies illustrate how Earned Value Management (EVM) has been applied in real-world projects across different industries to monitor performance, control costs, and ensure project success. By leveraging EVM techniques, project managers can make informed decisions, identify potential risks, and take timely corrective actions to achieve project objectives.

Chapter 8: Conclusion and Next Steps

In the final chapter, we'll recap key learnings from the book and discuss next steps for furthering your expertise in EVM. Whether you're looking to pursue certifications, engage in additional training, or apply EVM in your professional practice, this chapter will provide guidance on how to continue your journey in mastering EVM

Finally, we'll provide a curated list of resources, including books, articles, online courses, and software tools, to support your ongoing learning and practice of EVM. These resources will serve as valuable references as you continue to explore and apply EVM in your projects.

Get ready to unlock the power of Earned Value Management and elevate your project management skills to new heights! Let's begin our journey together.

Conclusion:

Earned Value Management (EVM) is a powerful project management technique that provides valuable insights into project performance by integrating cost, schedule, and scope metrics. Through the use of key performance indicators such as Schedule Variance (SV), Cost Variance (CV), Cost Performance Index (CPI), and Schedule Performance Index (SPI), project managers can effectively monitor progress, identify deviations from the plan, and take timely corrective actions to ensure project success.

By implementing EVM, organisations can:

- Gain visibility into project performance.
- Identify risks and issues early.
- Make informed decisions based on accurate data.
- Optimise resource utilisation.
- Improve project forecasting and budgeting.

Next Steps:

After understanding the fundamentals of EVM and its application in real-world scenarios, there are several next steps you can take to further enhance your skills and proficiency in EVM:

> EVM Certification: Consider pursuing EVM certifications such as the Project Management Professional (PMP) or Earned Value Management Professional (EVMP) certification offered by professional organisations like the Project Management Institute (PMI). These certifications validate your expertise in EVM and demonstrate your commitment to professional development.

By taking these next steps, you can further develop your proficiency in Earned Value Management (EVM) and position yourself as a skilled and knowledgeable project management professional capable of delivering successful projects in diverse industries and environments.

Resources and Tools and examples

Here are some resources and tools that can be valuable for learning about Earned Value Management (EVM) and implementing it effectively:

1. Books:

- "A Guide to the Project Management Body of Knowledge (PMBOK Guide)" by Project Management Institute (PMI): Provides a thorough overview of EVM concepts and techniques within the broader context of project management.

2. Professional Organisations:

- Project Management Institute (PMI): Offers resources, webinars, and networking opportunities related to EVM through its Practice Standard for Earned Value Management and Earned Value Management Community of Practice.
- Association for the Advancement of Cost Engineering (AACE): Provides resources and publications on cost engineering, including EVM-related topics.

4. Software Tools:

- Microsoft Project: A popular project management software that includes built-in EVM features for tracking project schedules, costs, and performance metrics.
- Primavera P6: A comprehensive project management tool with advanced EVM capabilities, ideal for managing large-scale projects and portfolios.

By leveraging these resources and tools, you can further enhance your understanding of Earned Value Management (EVM) and develop the skills necessary to effectively implement EVM techniques in your projects.

Printed in Great Britain
by Amazon

45077634R00020